BRAIN BOOSTERS
NUMBER PUZZLES

ARCTURUS

ARCTURUS

This edition published in 2017 by Arcturus Publishing Limited
26/27 Bickels Yard, 151–153 Bermondsey Street,
London SE1 3HA

ISBN: 978-1-78428-485-5
CH005337NT
Supplier 29, Date 0817, Print run 5783

Written by Lisa Regan
Illustrated by Ed Myer and Graham Rich
Designed by Trudi Webb
Edited by Lisa Regan and Joe Harris

Printed in China

TIPS ON NUMBER PUZZLES FROM SIR COUNTALOT

Read the instructions before you start. Some puzzles have more than one step.

Use your times tables to help you. They make things a lot easier!

Keep a pen and paper for making notes as you go. It is much easier to do this than to try to remember all the numbers along the way.

There are lots of different types of puzzles in this book! Challenge yourself with counting puzzles, multiplying and dividing questions, and logic tests. Which puzzles do you like best?

FLAMINGO FUN

How many flamingoes can you count? 5

And how many legs must there be?

If each flamingo eats 3 shrimps, how many shrimps is that? 45

This number-bot loves to play with numbers. Every number that enters his machine goes through three steps: First multiply by 2, then add 2, then divide by 2.

Number 6 enters the machine:
$6 \times 2 + 2 \div 2 = 7$

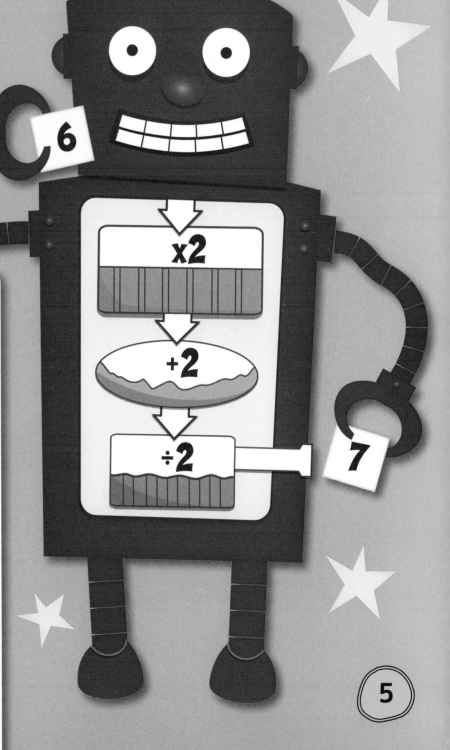

Number-bot

6

x2

+2

÷2

7

What will happen to the following numbers?

a 8 /9   b 10 /11

c 12 /13   d 14 /15

Look at what happens to the numbers after they have been through the machine. Can you see a pattern in the sequence of the answers?

5

SIR COUNTALOT

Sir Countalot is home from a number quest! Can you circle all the numbers in the 6 times table on the flags?

These four friends are having pizza. Read the clues then look at the pizzas to figure out which pizza belongs to which child.

PIZZA NIGHT!

Roxanne

Freddie

1. Mario has eaten ½ of his pizza.
2. Freddie has ½ mushroom and ½ cheese.
3. Roxanne has only eaten ⅛ of her pizza so far.
4. Lola has eaten ¼ of her pizza.

Mario

E

A

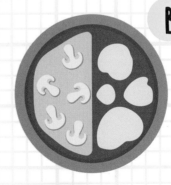

B

Lola

A

C

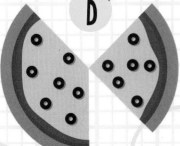

D

E

F

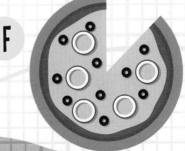

Fruit Stall

BANANAS: 2.50 A BUNCH

APPLES: 4 FOR 1.00

ORANGES: 3 FOR 1.50

WATERMELON: 3.00 EACH

PLUMS: 8 FOR 1.00

STRAWBERRIES: 2.00 A BOX

GRAPES: 1.75 A BUNCH

PINEAPPLE: 3.50 EACH

How much would each of these
fruit baskets cost at
Mr. Appleton's fruit stall?

B =6.75

1.75

3.00

2.00

350

A

7.00

250

1.00

C =5.00

D

1.75
1.00
2.50
———
5.25

E = 6.00

Which is
the most
expensive
basket?

GONE BANANAS!

Put the monkeys into pairs, so that each pair has a different prime number of bananas. 1,3,5,7 √1,13

PLANET HOPPING

Guide the astronaut through space to the big purple planet, stopping at the planets that continue the number sequence.

START

1

3

10

18

6

12

15

21

22

30

46

17

28

30

25

36

26

FINISH

44

38

45

55

BUILDING BRICKS

Beth the builder needs each vehicle to carry a load of 20 bricks to the building site. Match each vehicle with the correct load, so that they all have 20 bricks.

1 = C
2 = B
3 = D
4 = B
5 = A

CONE CONFUSION

Guide Beth back to the site, touching all the cones that follow the nine times table.

108 82 81 72 70

90 54 63 62

99

45

56 36 27

38 24 13 18

30 9

START

HUNGRY BEAR PAIRS

Pair up each bear with the right honey pot. The numbers on every bear and honey pot must add up to 50.

A 15

B 26

Mmm honey!!

D

31

E

42

C
Yum!

7

1 B 24

2 C 43

3 E 8

4 D 19

5 A 35

These squirrels have all been gathering acorns, ready for the winter.

Which squirrel has collected the most?

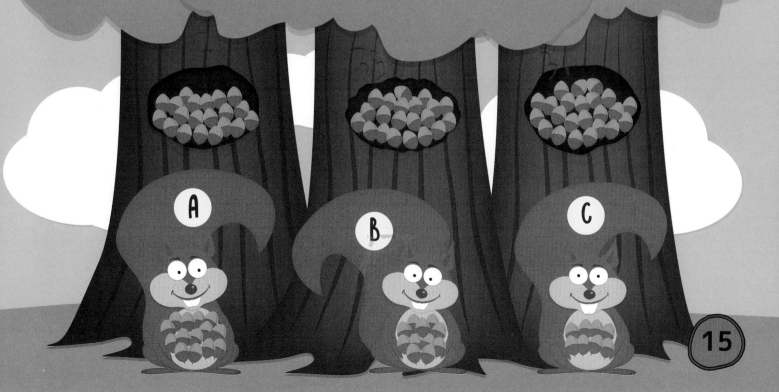

A

B

C

15

BETTY'S BAKERY

Fill in the missing numbers in Betty's window display. The number on the top cake will tell you how many cupcakes she has sold today!

320

135   185

48   67   98

29   40

12   22   36   4

Add numbers next to each other to give the number above.

Read the clues and solve the problems to figure out where each car finished in the race.

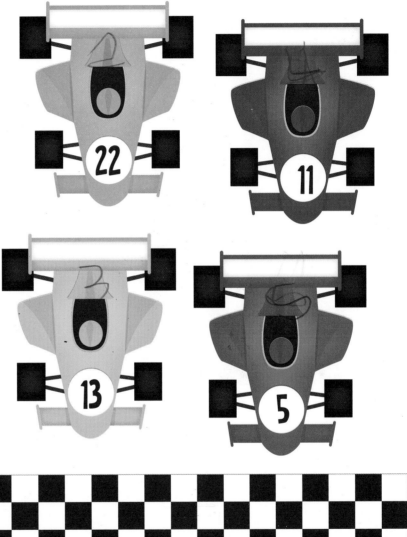

1. The winning car's number = 7x7. =49
2. Solve this problem to find second place: (8 + 3) x 2 = ? =22
3. The car in third place is the sixth prime number. =13
4. The car in fourth place is half of the second place car's number. 11
5. Solve this problem to find out which car finished last: 25 ÷ 5 = ? 5

SCHOOL OF FISH

Professor Ink Pot is teaching his pupils the times tables. They must collect all the bubbles with numbers that appear in the 7 times table. Can you help them?

Sir Countalot's faithful hound, Henry, is always by his side. Sir Countalot's ancestors all had dogs, and here they are! Which hound lived the longest?

BRUISER

1916-1930

HORACE

1750-1765

PERCY

1935-1943

FLUFFKIN

1889-1900

SNOOZER

1975-1987

HATTIE

1640-1649

NUMBER-BOTS

Each number-bot has a different function. Fill in the missing numbers. What number is input to give the answer for each bot?

Ben is bug spotting.

BUG SPOTTING

Help him to fill in his tally chart.

FIRST PLACE

Mario, Freddie, Roxanne, and Lola have all taken part in a competition.

The friends have scored points for each event in which they took part. Look at the points board and the results.

	Points for 1st place	Points for 2nd place	Points for 3rd place	Points for 4th place
100m Sprint	100	75	50	25
Hurdles	80	60	40	20
Long jump	150	100	75	25

	100m Sprint	Hurdles	Long jump	
Mario	3rd place 50	4th place 20	1st place 150	= 220
Freddie	4th place 25	2nd place 75	2nd place 100	= 200
Roxanne	1st place 100	1st place 80	4th place 25	= 205
Lola	2nd place 75	3rd place 40	3rd place 75	= 190

1 Which friend scored the highest number of points to win the overall winner's trophy? Mario

BEAR'S SUPPER

Help this hungry bear catch his fish supper! Guide him through the river, only catching the fish with numbers that are multiples of 8.

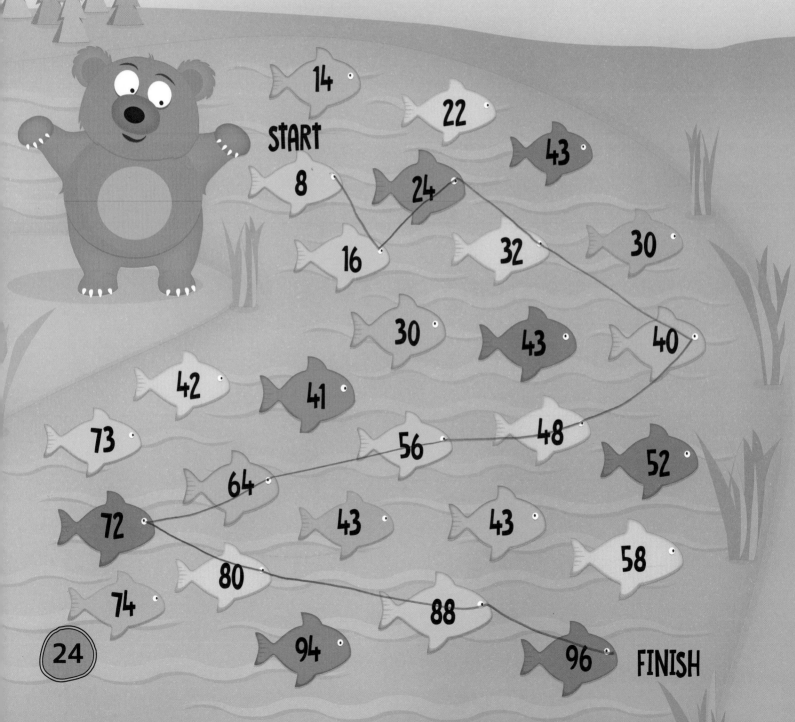

24

WHOSE POOCH?

Find the answers to the number problems to match each pooch to its rightful owner.

18 + 19

39

50 - 17

38

37

33

13 × 3

76 ÷ 2

HUNGRY BUNNIES

How many carrots will each bunny eat if they share them equally?

4

Sudoku-bot

Fill in the numbers on this Sudoku-bot's display so that each row, column and mini-grid contains the numbers 1 to 6.

5					2
	2		4	3	
					1
2					
	1	3		2	
					4

PENNY'S PET STORE

Penny's Pet Store is the best in town.

OPEN

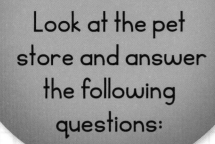

Look at the pet store and answer the following questions:

2

Penny sells two rabbits and buys four more. How many rabbits does she now have?

7

1

Add the number of cats to the number of birds. What is the result?

6

4

The green fish has ten babies. The others have six babies each. How many fish are there altogether? 32

3

Half of the hamsters are female. Each has six babies. How many hamsters are there now? 30

Counting Sheep

Help Farmer Fergus to round up his flock into their pens. All the sheep with even numbers go on the left and all the sheep with odd numbers go on the right.

14

13

5

33

8

26

25

4

37

How many sheep will there be in each pen?

30

15

9

29

Dino Plates

Look at the Stegosaurus plates. Which dinosaur has plates which add up to 5 x 5?

FAIRY FOURS

Help Flora the Fairy to collect all the stars with numbers that can be divided by 4.

44   30   24   38

26

42   20   36   28

12   4   8   16

22   40

5   22   11

14   32

Friends Mario, Freddie, Roxanne, and Lola all have slightly different ages. Solve the sums to figure out the age of each friend.

ROXANNE'S AGE IS $\frac{3}{4}$ OF THE NUMBER 16

12

FREDDIE'S AGE IS $3\frac{1}{2} + 4\frac{1}{4} + 3\frac{1}{4}$

11

MARIO'S AGE IS $4\frac{3}{4} + 5\frac{1}{4}$

10

LOLA'S AGE IS $6\frac{1}{2} + 6\frac{1}{2}$ *13*

SIR COUNTALOT'S COMPETITION

Sir Countalot's Knight Competition has been a great success. In which order did the knights finish?

Find the following numbers inside the number-bot:

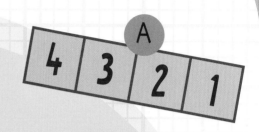

A
| 4 | 3 | 2 | 1 |

4	7	8	1	8	5	2	3	2
5	4	9	6	7	1	8	4	2
4	2	2	3	4	2	3	5	9
5	7	4	3	2	1	2	4	2
1	2	3	6	5	2	5	2	1
8	3	7	2	7	8	4	2	6
5	8	6	3	4	6	2	5	4
3	4	5	2	3	3	4	7	6
6	3	4	7	3	3	2	5	2

B
| 6 | 4 | 6 | 2 |

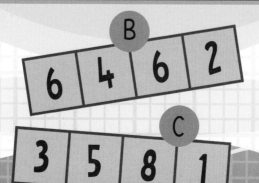

C
| 3 | 5 | 8 | 1 |

35

BLAST OFF!

Which rocket is moving at the greatest speed? Solve the rocket puzzles to find out!

A 101 x 2

B 210 − 10

C 10 x 20

Guide Frank the Frog across the lily pads, leaping only on the lily pads which continue the number sequence.

LILY PAD LEAP

Take Five

Guide Gina through the site, counting up in fives until she reaches the house she is building.

5	10	12	14	23	29	19	
2	6	8	15	20	25	27	36	20
31	46	49	44	32	30	32	33	30
50	51	50	45	40	35			
56	53	55	42	47	49			
		60	65	70	72	74	76	81
62	64	62	66	75		77	79	83
90	88	84	85	80	81	83	85	86
			90	92	94	99	90	
93	91	94	95	99	98	108	109	
	94		100	105	110	115		

38

Gina and her team have been joined by the mayor at the opening of their new glass building.

New Building

Add numbers next to each other to fill in the answer above and complete the pyramid.

620

310 310

170 140 170

100 70 70 100

60 40 30 **40** **60**

35 25 15 **15** 25 35

20 **15** **10** 5 **10** **15** 20

FAIRY DOOR

Flora has forgotten the magical code to her fairy door! Solve the clues to figure out the four numbers in the code for her.

Number 1:
The number of hours in a day divided by 4.

Number 2:
The number of months in a year divided by 4.

Number 3:
The number of tentacles on two octopuses, divided by 4.

Number 4:
The number of legs on a spider divided by 4.

6 3 4 2

Half the Fun

Help Professor Ink Pot to find the starfish number pairs. Match each starfish he is holding with the one that is exactly half its number on the ocean floor.

ODD SOCKS

Pair all of the socks by pattern. The numbers on each pair add up to 50, except one. Which pair is different?

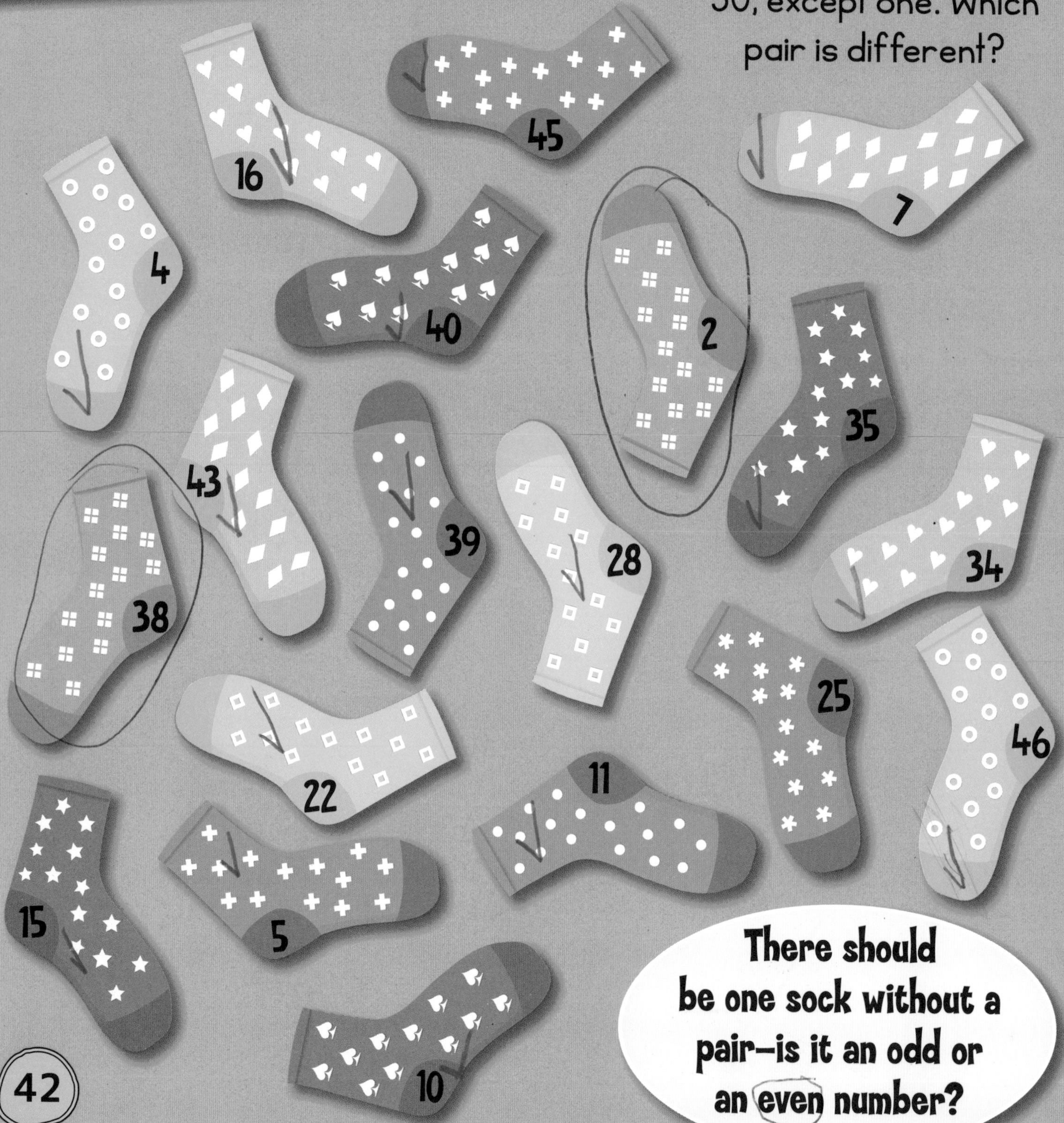

45

16

7

4

40

2

35

43

39

28

34

38

22

25

46

15

5

11

10

There should be one sock without a pair—is it an odd or an even number?

A Piece of Cake

Betty has had another busy day at the bakery. She needs to write down how much is left of each cake. Match the cakes above to the fractions below.

SPORTS FUN

Write the correct number next to each picture, using the clues to help you. If you get them all right, each row, column and diagonal set of three numbers will add up to 15.

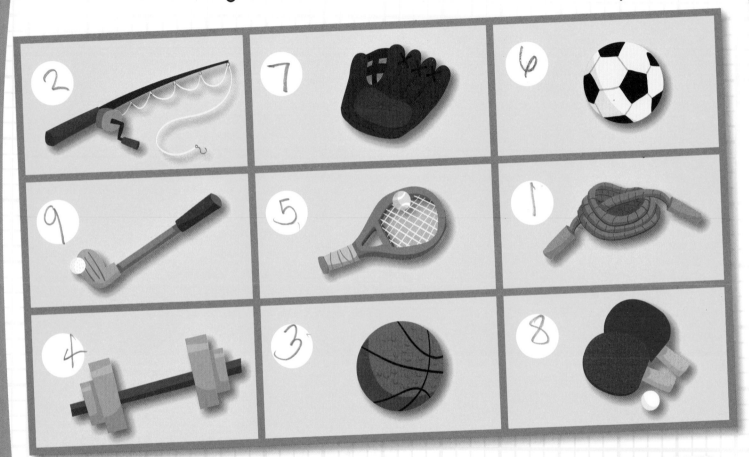

1. Jump with this to get fit.
2. Use it for angling.
3. Throw it through a hoop.
4. Pretty heavy stuff!
5. This sport has aces!
6. Usually kicked by 22 players.
7. Very handy for catching.
8. A sport played on a table.
9. A sport featuring eagles and birdies.

ROCK OF AGES

Use the clues to work out the age of each member of the Crag family. Hint: All their ages are even numbers.

CLUES

The mother is three times the age of her daughter and two years younger than her husband.

The father is more than 20 years older than his daughter.

The son is the youngest, and is one quarter of his dad's age.

BRAIN FOOD

Each of these treats represents a number: 2, 3, 5 or 8. Work out the value of each to make the subtraction work.

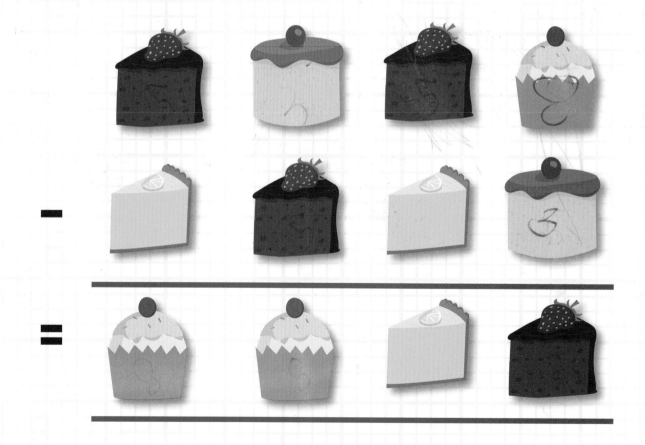

QUACK QUACK

Match each duckling with its mother by adding the lily pad numbers together to make 50 each time.

FLYING HIGH

Figure out the number pattern on each flying thing, and work out what number replaces the question mark for each one.

A

4
7
13
25
? 49

B

3
8
18
33
53
? 78

C

6 +2
8 +1
9 +0.5
9.5 +0.25
9.75 +
?

Each of these sea creatures represents a different number. What are their values? The numbers outside the grid are the sum of each row or column.

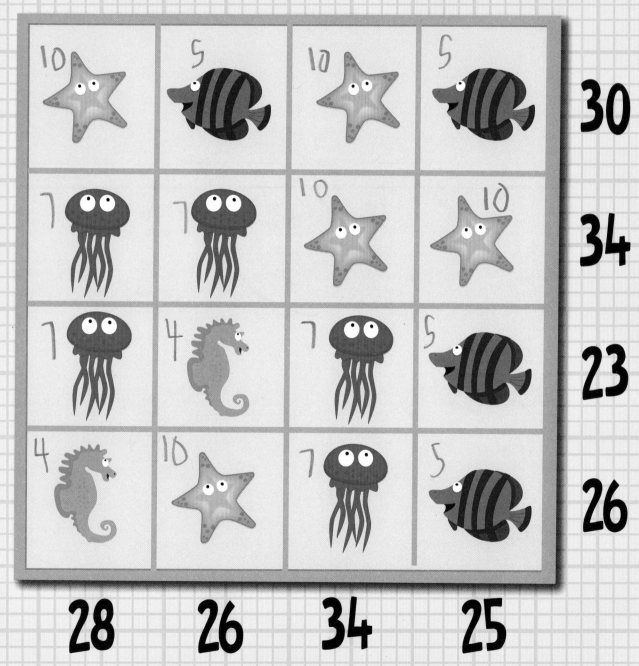

10	5	10	5	30
7	7	10	10	34
7	4	7	5	23
4	10	7	5	26
28	26	34	25	

49

SUDOKU-BOT

Fill in the numbers on this Sudoku-bot's display so that each row, column and mini-grid contains the numbers 1 to 6.

3	4	6	2	5	1
5	1	2	3	6	4
4	2	5	1	3	6
1	6	3	4	2	5
2	5	4	6	1	3
6	3	1	5	4	2

50

Number Jigsaw

Shade any shape that contains an even number to reveal a picture.

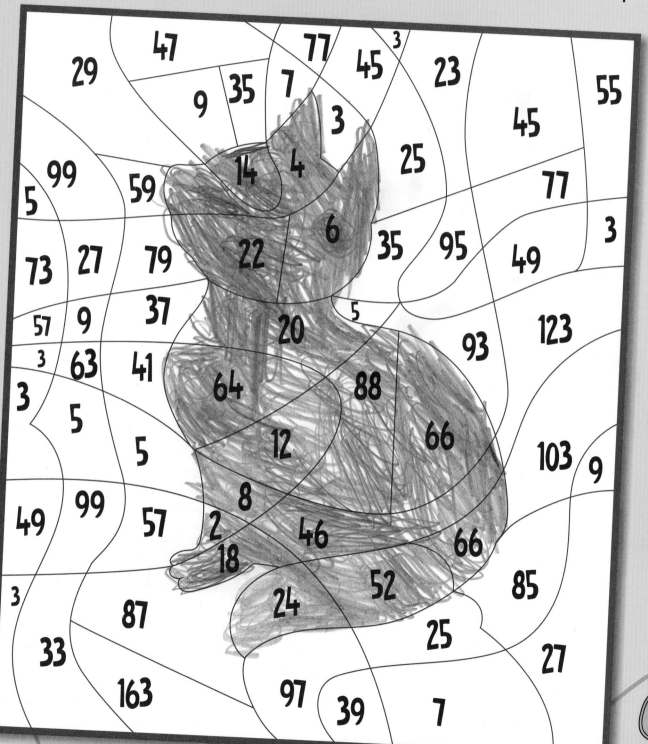

29 47 77 45 3 23 55
9 35 7 45
3 25
99 59 14 4 77
5 6 35 95 49 3
73 27 79 22
37 5 20 93 123
57 9
3 63 41 64 88 66
3 5 12 103 9
5 66
49 99 57 8 46 66
2 18 52 85
3 24
87 25 27
33 163 97 39 7

TOWER TOTALS

What fraction needs to appear in the lowest window to make a total of 2? Work it out to rescue the children stuck at the top of the tower.

$$\frac{7}{8}$$

+

$$\frac{1}{4}$$

+

$$\frac{3}{8}$$

+

? ½ ½

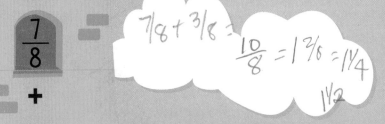

$7/8 + 3/8 = \frac{10}{8} = 1\frac{2}{8} = 1\frac{1}{4}$

$1\frac{1}{2}$

Match each child to his or her sandcastle by working out the answer to each problem.

BODMAS

multiplication

subtraction

brackets | division | addition

order
of
operations

(3 × 3) + 5

(8 ÷ 2) + 12

(4.5 × 2) + 9

20 − (0.5 × 10)

18

16

15

14

FEEDING TIME

Penny needs to make sure her animals are all well fed. Work out how much food she needs.

BIRD SEED
Contents:
600 spoonfuls

REPTILE FOOD
Contents:
60 scoops

RABBIT FOOD
Contents:
50 cups

FISH FOOD
Contents:
156 servings

1 Each rabbit eats half a cup of food per day. How many days before the container is empty? 2 days

2 The iguana is only fed on Tuesdays and Fridays. It eats one scoop of food each time. For how many weeks does one container last? 30 weeks

3 The fish need one serving of food each, three times a week. How many containers of food are needed in one year? 156

4 The birds are fed twice a day. Each is given three spoonfuls of seed each time. How much food do they need per week? 200

TIMESSSSS TABLESSSSSS

Each snake features numbers from a different times table. Can you work out what they are?

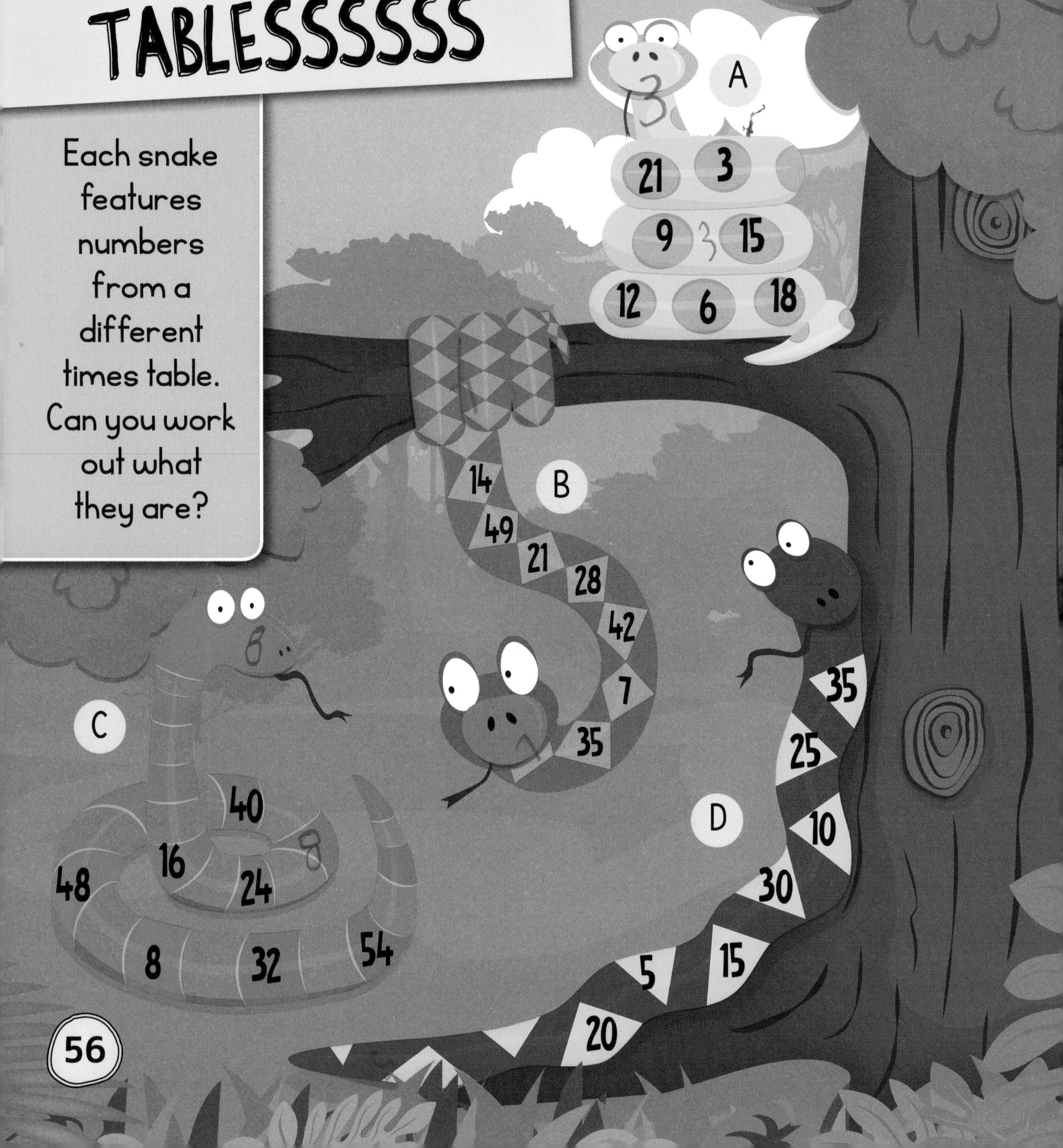

A

21 3
9 3 15
12 6 18

B

14
49
21
28
42
7
35

C

40
16
48 24
8 32 54

D

35
25
10
30
5 15
20

56

BULLSEYE

Which of the archers has scored the most?

White scores
2 points

Black scores
4 points

Blue scores
6 points

Red scores
8 points

Gold scores
15 points

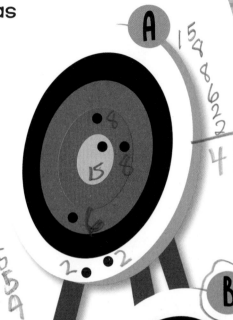

A

```
  15
  4
  8
  6
  2 2
 ----
  41
```

B

```
 15
 15
 4
 6
 6
 8
 ----
 54
```

C

```
 15
 6
 8
 6
 6
 6
 6
 15
```

SUNFLOWER SUMS

Add together the numbers on each sunflower's leaves. Which leaf must you prune from each to get the correct total, shown on the flower?

58

Share out the jewels so that each queen receives four red rubies, six green emeralds, and two blue sapphires.

A

B

C

D

E

F

G

H

I

SPACE FLIGHT

Can you spot the alien hiding in B3? There are five more aliens in this scene. Find the co-ordinates for all of them.

Stepping Stones

Help Davy across the river, walking on all of the stepping stones that contain numbers divisible by 5.

77

46

25

51

40

93

53

15

31

61

20

67

37

12

75

23

57

46

35

28

55

Ugg's Eggs

Number of miles

Ugg has gathered enough eggs to last his family for days. Work out how many miles he has walked by filling in the numbers.

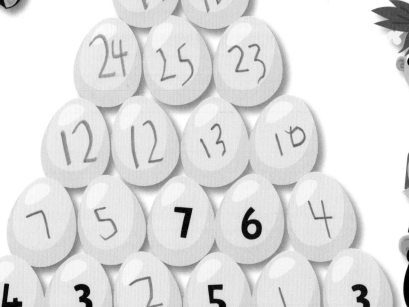

97

49 · 48

24 · 25 · 23

12 · 12 · 13 · 10

7 · 5 · 7 · 6 · 4

4 · 3 · 2 · 5 · 1 · 3

Hint:
Add two numbers next to each other to fill in the egg above.

SEEING DOUBLE

9	2	4	9	3	9	7	2	9
2	3	9	8	9	3	3	9	2
7	2	3	4	3	2	4	8	3
2	9	0	3	9	3	3	8	8
3	4	7	2	9	3	9	3	3
2	3	2	3	7	3	3	2	4
3	6	4	3	9	4	9	4	8
7	3	7	3	2	4	3	4	9
9	2	9	3	4	3	2	9	3

Double the number in the box, and then double it again and again. Can you find each of the three answers hidden in the grid?

247
x2
494
x2
988
x2
1976

63

Building Bonds

Multiply together the numbers on the wheels to find out the load each vehicle can carry. Work out which number replaces the question mark each time.

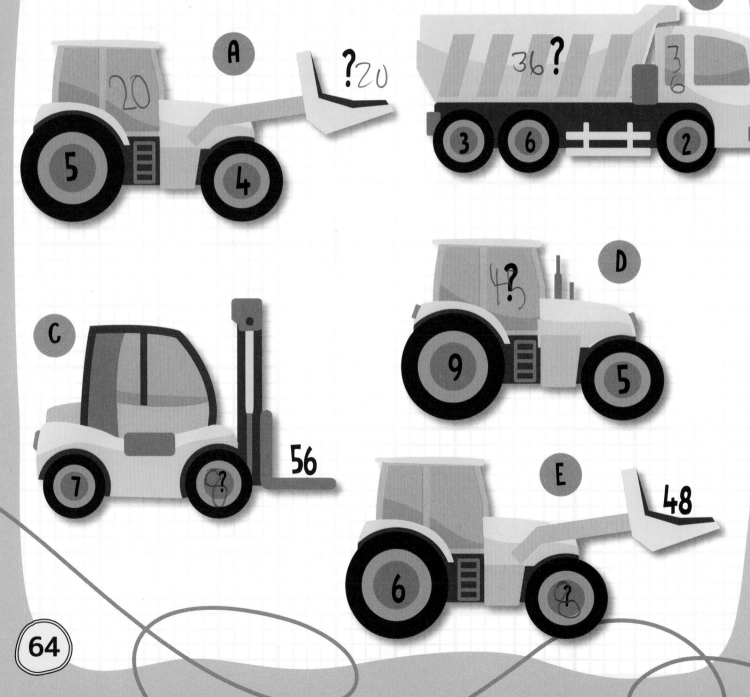

A

? 20

B

36 ?

3
6

3   6   2

C

56

7   ?

D

4 ?

9   5

E

48

6   ?

PINK PAIRS

Put the flamingoes into pairs by matching the fractions that are the same. Which flamingo is on its own?

TREASURE HUNT

Find a way to the treasure at the bottom of the ocean, stopping at the fish that follow the number pattern.

DE-BUGGED

Decode the problems using the bug code, and then draw in the answers for yourself. You can use two bugs to make a number, for example two bees = 66.

a 🐞 + 🦋 = 14

b 🐝 × 🕷 = 8

c 🦋 + 🦋 + 🐞 = 15

d (🕷 + 🦋) × 🕷 = 14

e (🐝 + 🦋 + 🦋) ÷ 🕷 = 6

🦋 = 1   🕷 = 2   🪱 = 4

🦋 = 5   🐝 = 6   🐞 = 9

SPOT THE SHEEP

Which of the sheep does not have a number that is divisible by 6?

Each sea creature represents the number 2, 5, 7, or 9. Work out which picture is which number to make the subtraction work.

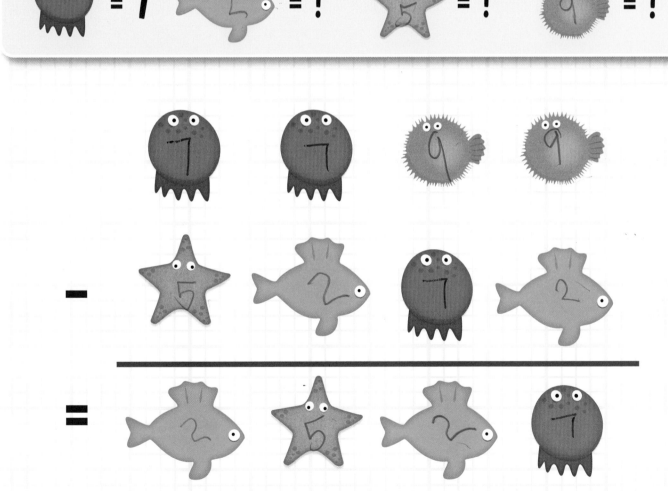

SUPER JUICE

The children are mixing juice drinks to try new tastes. Help them work out their recipes.

1. The jug of orange holds as much as the other jugs added together.
2. The small jugs each hold 2 full glasses of juice.
3. Each recipe mixes two types of juice in one glass, half and half.
4. There are eight children with a glass each.

How many of the glasses must contain orange juice?

Each yellow rabbit takes three carrots. The others share the carrots that are left. How many carrots does each brown rabbit have?

Bunny Feast

Build It Up

Place the four mathematical symbols + - x ÷ onto the blank cones to make the problem work out properly, moving from left to right across the page.

50 ___ 2 ___ 5 ___ 18 ___ 4 = 48

72

IT'S A WILD LIFE

Write the correct number next to each picture, using the clues to help you. If you get them all right, each row, column, and diagonal set of three numbers will add up to 15.

1. A black and white creature.
2. This creature can fly.
3. Loves to eat bamboo.
4. A bear that can swim.
5. An animal with stripes.
6. A meat eater from Africa.
7. It is striped and has a mane.
8. It keeps its baby in a pouch.
9. An animal with horns on its nose.

Be a numbers whizz and work out the answers to the racing problems.

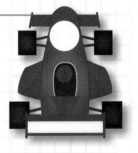

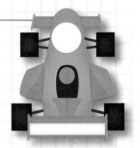

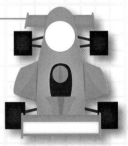

1

If the race takes two hours to finish 80 laps, how many laps will the drivers have done after 30 minutes? 20

2

The driver who starts in eighth position overtakes five cars. What position does he finish in? 3

BUSY BEES

Pair up the honey pots that have the same number of bees around them. Which of the pots does not form part of a pair? F

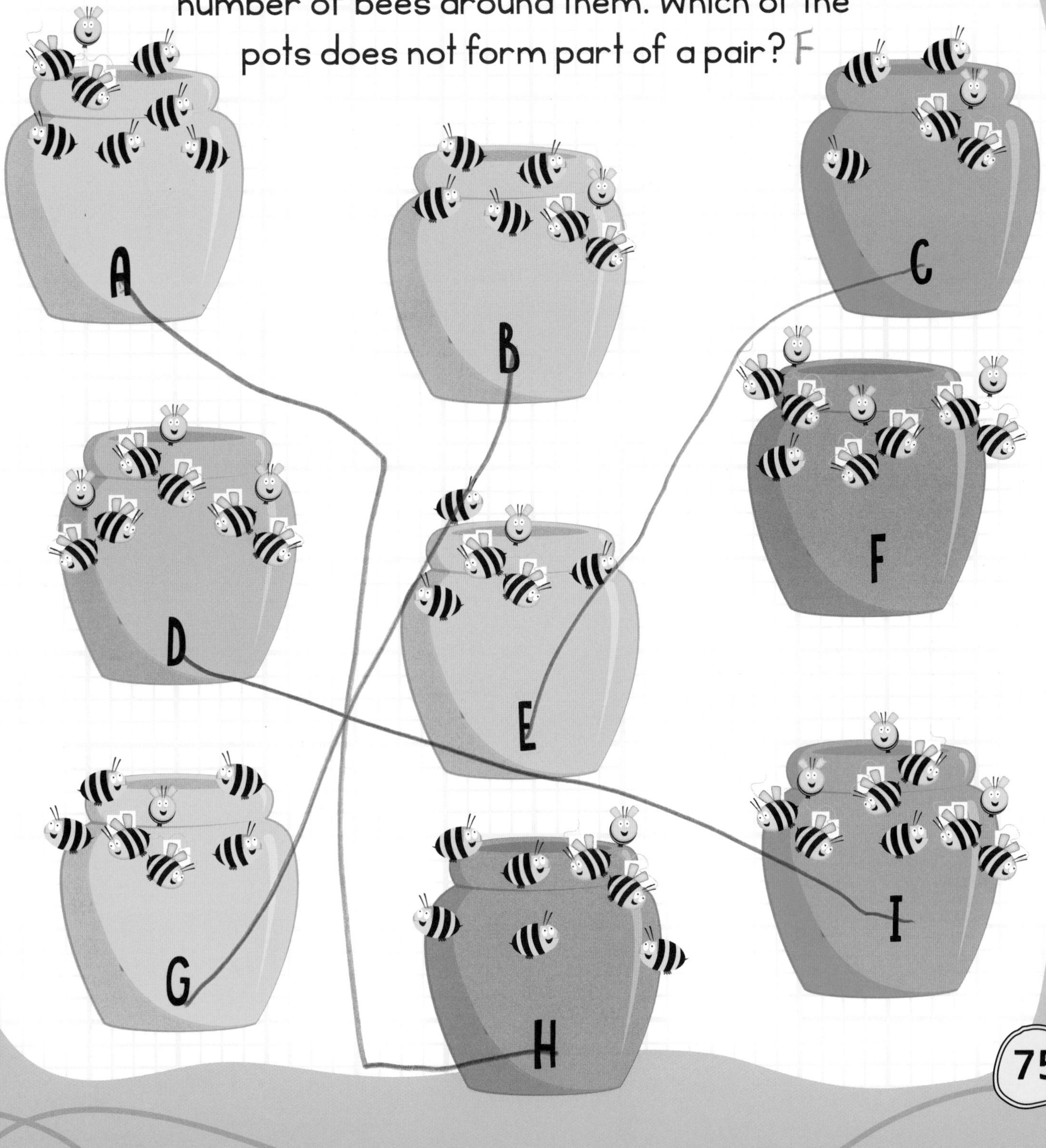

A

B

C

D

E

F

G

H

I

PORTRAIT GALLERY

Take a look at the paintings and work out the answers to the questions.

Colin Quicksilver
1829-1875

*6

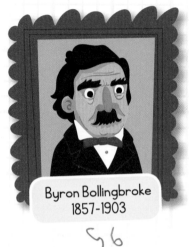

Byron Bollingbroke
1857-1903

56

Violet Brumby-Winstone
1912-1950

38

Caitlin Midwinter
1832-1925

93

Empress Frances III
1934-1977

43

Xavier Delarue
1906-1959

53

1. Who lived for the longest time? Caitlin midwinter
2. Who was born first? Colin Quicksilver
3. Who died at the age of 43? Empress Frances III
4. Who died in their sixth decade? Xavier Delarue

Flower Factors

Which of the numbers on the leaves of each sunflower does not divide exactly into the number on the flower?

HEALTHY SNACKS

Count the fruit items and use your times tables to work out the answers to the questions.

1. How many apples in 4 baskets? 28
2. How many strawberries in 6 boxes? 18
3. How many bananas in 8 bunches? 24
4. How many oranges in 3 baskets? 15
5. How many grapes in 5 bunches? 55

ROUND AND ROUND

Fit the numbers from 1 to 7 into the empty circles once each so that each straight line of three numbers adds up to the same total.

OOH LA LA!

The friends are visiting Paris and buying souvenirs. Help them work out this problem.

Roxanne and Mario buy two models of the Eiffel Tower and one of the Arc de Triomphe. They spend 8 Euros.

Lola and Freddie buy three models of the Eiffel Tower and two of the Arc de Triomphe. It costs them 13 Euros.

If Freddie wants to buy an extra Eiffel Tower for his brother, how much money will he need?

HARD CHEESE!

Before Mister Mouse can begin nibbling, help him to fill the holes with numbers from the doorway to his house. The numbers on each piece of cheese should total the same.

23
16
5   8
18
22
12

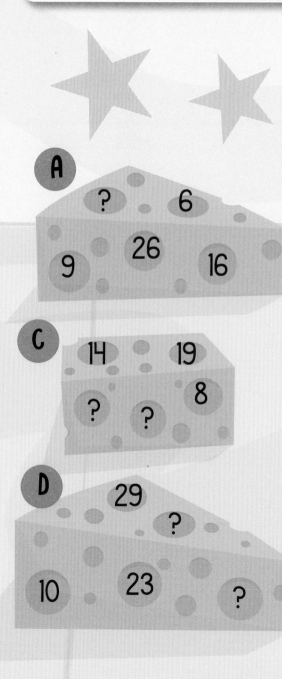

A
?   6
26
9   16

B
33   4
?   7
15

C
14   19
?   ?   8

D
29
?
10   23   ?

E
13   2
31   6   ?

WIN A PRIZE!

The school fundraiser has a prize for anyone who can guess the number of marbles in the jar. See if you can work out how many there are.

No one guesses exactly right, but the five nearest guesses are 50, 53, 62, 66, and 71. Of these guesses, one is 1 out, one is 3 out, one is 8 out, one is 10 out, and one is 13 out. How many marbles are in the jar? 63

Bank Raid

Use the clues to work out the four-digit number that opens the safe.

All the digits are different.

It begins and ends with even numbers.

The two middle numbers are both odd.

It is exactly divisible by both 26 and 106.

TAKE AIM

Sir Countalot has decided to test his talents at archery. How does he score each of the totals, using six arrows every time?

a. Total score 30

b. Total score 41

c. Total score 47

d. Total score 70

White scores
2 points

Black scores
4 points

Blue scores
6 points

Red scores
8 points

Gold scores
15 points

15
8
6
4
2

Help the children find a prize by popping the correct balloons. Any with a number divisible by nine contains a gift.

BANG!

45

61

16

57

54

48

19

27

36

24

38

Packing Up

Help Mrs. Payne work out what to take on the picnic. How many of each sandwich should she prepare?

2 cheese an

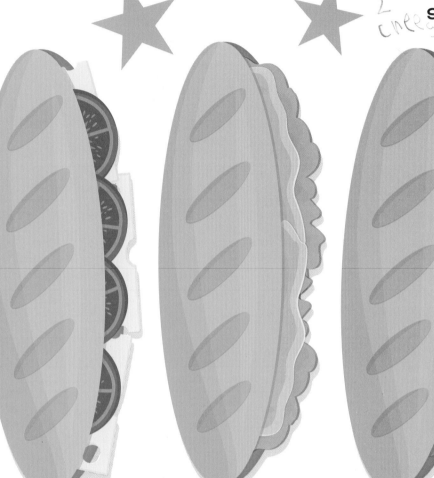

X2   X0   X0

Four people want a cheese and tomato sandwich, but only half each.

Two people want half a tuna and cucumber sandwich and half a ham and lettuce sandwich each.

Six people want a third of a tuna and cucumber sandwich and a third of a cheese and tomato sandwich each.

14. Hungry Bear Pairs
A = 5, B = 1, C = 2, D = 4, E = 3

15. Squirrels and Nuts
Squirrel A

16. Betty's Bakery
330 cakes

17. Racing Cars
1st place: 49
2nd place: 22
3rd place: 13
4th place: 11
5th place: 5

18. School of Fish

19. Hounds Through History
Horace lived the longest.

20. Number-bots
9 + 50 - 29 = 30
50 ÷ 2 × 3 = 75
10 × 5 + 4 = 54
6 + 4 × 6 = 60

21. Bug Spotting

🪰 = $\cancel{||||}\,|$
🦋 = $||||$
🐛 = $\cancel{||||}\,||$
🐝 = $\cancel{||||}\,|||$
🕷 = $\cancel{||||}\,\cancel{||||}\,|||$
🐞 = $\cancel{||||}$

22. First Place
Mario scored 220 points, Freddie scored 185 points, Roxanne scored 205 points, Lola scored 190 points. Mario won the trophy.

24. Bear's Supper

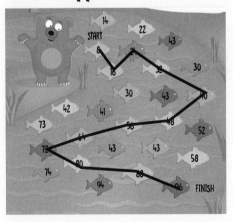

25. Whose Pooch?
18 + 19 = 37   50 - 17 = 33
13 × 3 = 39   76 ÷ 2 = 38

26. Hungry Bunnies
They have four carrots each (20 ÷ 5).

27. Sudoku-bot

5	3	4	1	6	2
1	2	6	4	3	5
3	6	5	2	4	1
2	4	1	6	5	3
4	1	3	5	2	6
6	5	2	3	1	4

28. Penny's Pet Store
1. 6
2. 7
3. 16
4. 32

30. Counting Sheep
There will be five sheep on the left and eight sheep on the right.

31. Dino Plates
C

32. Fairy Fours

33. Age Order
Roxanne is 12, Freddie is 11, Mario is 10, Lola is 13.

34. Sir Countalot's Competition
B. 300
C. 275
D. 250
A. 225

35. Number Search

4	7	8	1	8	5	2	3	2
5	4	9	6	7	1	8	4	2
4	2	2	3	4	2	3	5	9
5	7	4	3	2	1	6	4	2
1	2	3	6	5	2	5	2	1
8	3	7	2	7	8	4	2	6
5	8	6	3	4	6	2	5	4
3	4	5	2	3	3	4	7	6
6	3	4	7	3	3	2	5	2

36. Blast Off!
A

37. Lily Pad Leap
5, 10, 16, 21, 27, 32, 38, 43, 49, 54, 60, 65, 71, 76, 82
The sequence is:
+ 5 + 6 + 5 + 6

38. Take Five

5	10	12	14	23	29	19
2	6	8	15	20	25	27	36	20
31	46	49	44	32	30	32	33	30
50	51	50	45	40	35
56	53	55	42	47	49
60	65	70	72	74	76	81
62	64	62	66	75	77	79	83
90	88	84	85	80	81	83	85	86
90	92	94	99	90
93	91	94	95	99	98	108	109
94	100	105	110	115

39. New Building

40. Fairy Door
6342

41. Half the Fun
The number pairs are: 6 and 12, 10 and 20, 30 and 60, 100 and 200, 5 and 10, 25 and 50, 15 and 30, 50 and 100.

42. Odd Socks
The different pair has the numbers 38 and 2, which only adds up to 40.
The sock without a pair is an odd number: 25.

43. A Piece of Cake
A = 3/4
B = 1/8
C = 1/3
D = 3/8
E = 1/6
F = 1/2

44. Sports Fun

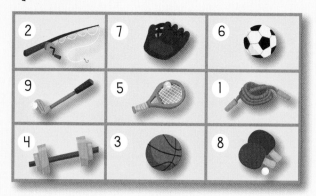

45. Rock of Ages
The mother is 30, the father is 32, the daughter is 10, and the son is 8.

46. Brain Food
= 2
= 5
= 3
= 8

47. Quack Quack
33 + 17, 28 + 22, 36 + 14, 26 + 24

48. Flying High
A. 49 (double the gap between each number)
B. 78 (add multiples of 5 each time, so +5, +10, +15 and so on)
C. 9.875 (half the gap between each number)

49. Ocean Explorer
= 5
= 7
= 10
= 4

50. Sudoku-bot

3	4	6	2	5	1
5	1	2	3	6	4
4	2	5	1	3	6
1	6	3	4	2	5
2	5	4	6	1	3
6	3	1	5	4	2

51. Number Jigsaw

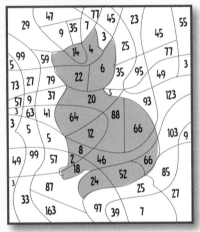

52. Tower Totals

1/2 (or 4/8)

53. At the Beach

(3 × 3) + 5 = 14

(8 ÷ 2) + 12 = 16

(4.5 × 2) + 9 = 18

20 - (0.5 × 10) = 15

54. Feeding Time

1. 20 days 2. 30 weeks 3. 4 containers
4. 126 spoonfuls

56. Timesssss Tablesssssss

A. 3x table

B. 7x table

C. 2x table, 4x table or 8x table

D. 5x table

57. Bullseye

B

58. Sunflower Sums

a. 15 b. 9 c. 13 d. 17 e. 7

59. Crown Jewels

The jewels should be split into three groups:

A, E, F

B, C, G

D, H, I

60. Space Flight

B3, D6, F7, G2, J1, J6

61. Stepping Stones

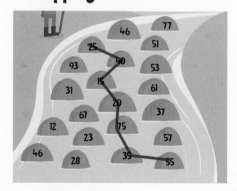

62. Ugg's Eggs

97 miles

63. Seeing Double

9	2	4	9	3	9	7	2	9
2	3	9	8	9	3	3	9	2
1	9	7	6	3	2	4	8	3
2	9	0	3	9	3	3	8	8
3	4	7	2	9	3	9	3	3
2	3	2	3	7	3	3	2	4
3	6	4	3	9	4	9	4	8
7	3	7	3	2	4	3	4	9
9	2	9	3	4	3	2	9	3

64. Building Bonds
A. 20   B. 36
C. 8   D. 45
E. 8

65. Pink Pairs
2/5 is on its own.
6/8 = 3/4
2/7 = 4/14
5/10 = 1/2
1/4 = 3/12

66. Treasure Hunt
1, 4, 8, 11, 15, 18, 22, 25, 29, 32
The sequence is:
+ 3 + 4 + 3 + 4

67. De-bugged
a. 🐛🐛🐛 🐛
b. 🐛🐛🐛 🕷
c. 🐛🐛🐛 🦋
d. 🐛🐛🐛 🐛
e. 🐝

68. Spot the Sheep
26

69. Deep Thoughts
🐙 = 7
🐟 = 2
⭐ = 5
🐡 = 9

70. Super Juice
All of the glasses have orange juice. There is enough orange juice for four full glasses, but each recipe contains half of one type of juice and half of another. So all eight glasses must contain orange juice.

71. Bunny Feast
Four carrots each

72. Build It Up
50 ÷ 2 + 5 - 18 × 4 = 48

73. It's a Wild Life

74. Race to the Finish
1. 20 laps
2. Third position

75. Busy Bees
D

76. Portrait Gallery
1. Caitlin Midwinter
2. Colin Quicksilver
3. Empress Frances III
4. Xavier Delarue

77. Flower Factors
A. 7   B. 9
C. 8   D. 8
E. 7

78. Healthy Snacks
1. 28
2. 18
3. 24
4. 15
5. 55

79. Round and Round
The central number is 7. The lines are:
1 + 7 + 6 = 14
2 + 7 + 5 = 14
3 + 7 + 4 = 14

80. Ooh La La!
3 Euros. Lola and Freddie buy an extra Tower and Arc, costing them 5 Euros more, meaning the price of a Tower and an Arc must add up to 5. The simplest way of solving this kind of puzzle is to guess at the prices for each item and work out how much the total would be. Then, make the prices larger or smaller depending on the answer.

81. Hard Cheese!
They should each add up to 75:
A. 18 B. 16 C. 22, 12 D. 5, 8 E. 23

82. Win a Prize!
63

83. Bank Raid
2756. (Multiply 26 and 106! These numbers do also go into other numbers, but those don't satisfy all the criteria.)

84. Take Aim
Here are some ways he could do it:
a. 30 = 2 + 2 + 4 + 6 + 8 + 8
b. 41 = 4 + 4 + 4 + 6 + 8 + 15
c. 47 = 4 + 6 + 6 + 8 + 8 + 15
d. 70 = 15 + 15 + 15 + 15 + 8 + 2

85. Bang!
Only four balloons have numbers from the 9 times table: 45, 54, 27, 36

86. Packing Up
Four cheese and tomato, three tuna and cucumber, and one ham and lettuce.

87. In the Balance
One zebra = two tigers, and one tiger = two kangaroos. So two zebras = eight kangaroos.

88. Who's There?
Bear is hiding!

89. Beat the Bots
B. + 6   C. - 10 D. + 4 E. x 2